FAQ

Frequently Asked Questions
about our beliefs,
practices, and principles

Copyright © 2017 by the Family Federation
for World Peace and Unification

Published by The Holy Spirit Association
for the Unification of World Christianity (HSA-UWC)

HSA-UWC
4 West 43rd Street, New York, NY 10036

ISBN: 978-1-931166-84-3

All rights reserved. No part of this publication may be reproduced, stored in a retrieval system or transmitted, in any form, or by any means, electronic, mechanical, recorded, photocopied, or otherwise, without the prior written permission of both the copyright owner and the above publisher of this book, except by a reviewer who may quote brief passages in a review.

The scanning, uploading, and distribution of this book via the Internet or via any other means without the permission of the publisher is illegal and punishable by law. Please purchase only authorized electronic editions and do not participate in or encourage electronic piracy of copyrightable materials. Your support of the author's rights is appreciated.

Printed in the United States of America

Contents

Foreword 5

Coolest Questions 6

Life, Death, Family, and Being Good 11
    Purpose of Life 11
    Family 12
    Morality 14
    Death and Eternal Life 16

God, Christ and the Second Advent 19
    Salvation and Resurrection 19
    Second Coming 20
    Jesus 22
    Messiah 25
    Heavenly Parent 26

Pillars of Unificationism 28
    Our Scriptures 28
    True Father Sun Myung Moon 29
    True Mother Hak Ja Han Moon 31
    True Parents 32
    Unification Church 34
    Family Federation for World Peace and Unification 36
    Marriage Blessing 38

Identity and Lifestyle 42
    About Unificationists 42
    Faith 44
    Religion 46
    Health and Spirituality 47
    Humanitarian Service and Reconciliation 48
    Peace Kingdom 51
    Politics 53
    Womanhood 54

Foreword

The FFWPU FAQ project was created in order to provide a centralized place for questions and answers about the teachings of Rev. and Mrs. Moon and the faith organization they founded. In a clear and transparent communication, we provide an overview of the beliefs, practices, and principles of the Unification movement.

The desire to create such a document sprung from the need to provide resources for the community as well as to harness the knowledge of the first generation of Unificationists, who spent decades studying and practicing the faith alongside Father and Mother Moon. We connected their heritage with the contemporary questions and challenges faced by the world today as articulated by the movement's second and third generations. It is a precious gift to be able to preserve these combined insights for the future.

The FAQ team worked with numerous consultants representing various Unification-based organizations and communities across the country. We hope this project will continue to grow and dig deeper and deeper in a way that will inspire and instruct generations to come.

Coolest Questions

Why are we born on this earth?

We are born on earth so that we can love as man and woman, have children, and build a wonderful world. God divided the male and female positions within Himself to create the physical world, and His complete self-expression was the first human ancestors. Seeing them brought Him enormous joy, and that joy was to expand infinitely through their multiplication of true children. Multiplication requires male and female in the physical world. As Jesus taught, marriage does not take place among angels "in the resurrection." This is one reason we are born on earth.

Another reason is, in Mother Moon's words, "God exists as an incorporeal being. He needs to assume a physical form through which to relate with the entire world of substance." God experiences joy as He senses and fashions the physical creation with us. In this, our joy is made complete.

Does faith in God make sense amidst so much suffering in the world?

Yes, faith in God does make sense, even in a world of suffering. God is your spiritual Parent. He grieves over the suffering in the world, and over the suffering each of us goes through. Nonetheless, God created you with your own portion of responsibility. He will not take that away from you. So He will not interfere with the choices you make, even if they are wrong choices that lead to suffering.

God does not whisk suffering away, but rather invests love and guidance. He hopes that you will choose just as He does—to bring happiness to others. When each of us fulfills our responsibility to live for the sake of others, we will not have the suffering we see today.

Why are there so many religions? How do we know which one is right?

There are many religions because God wanted to bring His ideals into diverse cultures. Adam and Eve's descendants scattered across the earth, developed different languages and character traits, and responded to God in different ways. God sent prophets and saints to every culture to found religions. He developed them through the original minds of those who sought the good.

Even though the expression of religious striving takes different forms, all religions share the same core elements and ideals. This is because the purpose underlying all religions is to seek the family that was lost in the Garden of Eden. Therefore, what makes a religion right is the degree to which it understands that God is our Parent and we are His children, and practices sacrificial love.

What happens to us after we die?

After we die, our finite body is given back to the earth and our spirit ascends to the spirit world, the eternal realm of love. Our passage into the spirit world is a new birth, like our arrival in this physical world from the womb. Our source of life on earth is air, sunlight and water, but in the spirit world, our source of life is love.

The quality of our life on earth determines our place in the spirit world. If we grow our spirit on earth through giving and receiving authentic love, we will find joy in heaven. We will meet the people whom we love and who love us, and experience eternal happiness together with God. If we live a selfish life on earth, we will not enjoy such happiness. God does not decide where we go in the spirit world; rather the way we live on earth determines our destination. Heaven and Hell are simply the realms closer to or further from God, our Heavenly Parent.

How do you explain the existence of God?

In a way consistent with the tenets of all faiths, we provide logical answers and practical answers to explain the existence of God. To answer logically, we refer to the order and beauty of creation and to the order and direction of human history.

Our practical answer is to believe that God exists and live based on that belief. Talk to God in prayer. Give of yourself for others. Practice your religion's spiritual disciplines, and study its spiritual teachings. Find a good mentor, and be a mentor to others. We think that your experiences will confirm God's existence.

Can we harmonize religion and science?

Through understanding God's principles by which He created the world, you can see within yourself the way to harmonize religion and science. You have two sides. One is the spiritual side that connects to religion. The other is the physical side that listens to science and understands the natural world. By connecting the spiritual and physical within you, you naturally will harmonize what you learn through religion and science.

Reverend Moon put this into practice on a larger level. He called scientists to apply spiritual values to their technical pursuits. He called them to apply a new ethic based on love for nature, respect for human beings, and a search for God. At the same time he called religious leaders to express their teachings in reasonable and plain language. He told them not to focus on their own religion's growth, but rather to serve other religions and the good of humankind.

Is Jesus going to come again? If so, how?

Yes, Jesus is going to come again. Jesus clearly foretold his return, and he said that its time, place and manner will be revealed to the faithful.

Jesus coming on the clouds is unacceptable to the scientific mind. Some believe that the Second Advent occurs whenever Jesus comes to dwell within the heart, but Jesus has been dwelling within the hearts of faithful believers for millennia. Others teach that the Second Coming is Jesus' return as a spirit, but Jesus has always visited Christians in the spirit.

Father Moon presents a biblical alternative. The prophet Malachi foretold that Elijah would come down from heaven, but Jesus said that John the Baptist was Elijah. In like manner, Christ could be born on earth. In fact, in the Bible, God never sent a person on the clouds. Every single prophet, saint, and the Messiah himself, was born on earth.

We believe the Second Coming will not be on the clouds, and is more than an event in the heart or in the spirit. To redeem our sins, Christ must come in the flesh, on the earth.

Do Unificationists believe we can end evil and corruption in this world?

Yes, we do. To overcome a world of evil and corruption God has revealed a new truth that embraces and harmonizes historical religions, science and philosophy, and allows all people to know the reality of God and life after death. When one feels the reality of God, the conscience comes alive and guides one on the path to happiness, free from sin and wrongdoing. This new truth, as taught by Father and Mother Moon, stands on the foundation of all religions.

What is a Unificationist?

We are people of faith working together to build a better world. We participate in Unification family churches and communities as well as in all the world's faith traditions. We come from all backgrounds, races, ethnicities and nationalities, and strive to live as one family under God. We believe that God called Rev. Sun Myung Moon and his wife, Dr. Hak Ja Han Moon, to bestow the Holy Marriage Blessing, which liberates us all to build ideal families for world peace. We honor the world's great scriptures, and view Reverend Moon's teachings as an expression of the principles and ideals common to them all.

What is unique about Unificationists?

We are unique in having a husband and wife as co-founders. Our mission is to save families, not just individuals. We are set apart by our understanding that God called Sun Myung Moon and Hak Ja Han Moon to be True Parents, and to bestow the Holy Marriage Blessing to committed men and women of all faith traditions, as the foundation for creating world peace through God-centered families.

We uphold God, the Creator, whose kingdom begins with the family. God's love is embodied in blessed marriages and families, which open the way to peaceful and prosperous communities, beyond religion, race and nationality.

Life, Death, Family, and Being Good

Purpose of Life

Do Unificationists believe there is a purpose to life?

Yes, we believe there is a purpose to each person's life. You are a beloved child of God, who created you and wants a relationship with you. The Divine Principle teaches that the ultimate purpose of your life is to receive and return joy and love to God. In Father Moon's words: "God's ultimate purpose for creating human beings is to experience joy through relating with ideal families filled with true love." And as does any parent of true love, God wants His children's joy to be greater than His own.

To give your Heavenly Parent, God, the greatest joy, God gave you three purposes to fulfill. These are in Genesis 1:28. The first is to be fruitful. To be fruitful is to grow and mature your individual mind, body, and soul in alignment with God's ideals. The second is to multiply. This means, upon the foundation of personal maturity, to marry and create a God-centered family. The third is to have dominion. To have dominion is to be a caretaker of the natural world, to offer your mind, soul, and talents to the world centered on true love.

Why are we born on this earth?

We are born so that we can love as man and woman, have children, and build a wonderful world. God divided the male and female positions within Himself to create the physical world, and His complete self-expression was the first human ancestors. Seeing them brought Him enormous joy, and that joy was to expand infinitely through their multiplication of true children. Multiplication requires male and female in the physical world. As Jesus taught, marriage does not take place among angels "in the resurrection." This is one reason we are born on earth. Another reason is, in Mother Moon's words, "God exists as an incorporeal being. He needs to assume a physical form through which to relate with the entire world of substance." God experiences joy as He senses and fashions the physical creation with us. In this, our joy is made complete.

Do Unificationists believe in predestination?

We believe in a form of predestination that allows for true freedom. We teach that God predestined His plan and principles, but does not know when each of us will practice those principles and fulfill that plan. "God determined when He created human beings that they accomplish the purpose of creation," but this "can be realized only when human beings complete their portion of responsibility." Once God's responsibility and our responsibility are accomplished together, we complete, in a process of "co-creation," the purpose for which God created us.

We affirm that our conscience tends toward God's goodness, and so it is predestined that "all people will gradually converge toward the goal of God's ideal world." This is the world of love of which humankind has dreamed since the beginning.

Family

Why do Unificationists consider the family so important?

We consider the family important for many reasons. We see the family as a microcosm of the world. It is the meeting point of past, present and future, and a textbook of love. By loving and valuing our family, we learn how to love and value people all around the world.

The family is the most important foundation for health, happiness and prosperity. Strong families are the key to peaceful communities and a beautiful world. Most important of all, the family is the place where God wants to dwell with His children on earth.

Are husbands and wives equally important to the family?

We see the loving presence of a husband and wife as equally essential to the well-being of the family. They are the center of the family. They represent the male and female image of God to their children. Each parent conveys a unique and irreplaceable substance of love. Children need both sides of our Creator's love to develop a balanced character, and this comes mainly through the parents.

The parents' example of unity with each other and unchanging love for their children is passed on generation after generation. The roles of the husband and wife are fundamental to a home where God is present and where all family members find joy, friendship, support and security.

Do Unificationists believe in the equality of men and women?

Yes, we believe that we, as men and women, have equal value and importance to God, to each other, and to the world. This understanding of our equality stems from the marriage relationship. In a marriage, male and female partners complete each other, for only in our union do we resemble the image of God. In bestowing this gift of completion upon our spouse, we men and women are absolutely equal in value.

Upon this foundation, Father Moon stated that we share the same position, rank, inheritance and ownership, and have the right to accompany each other and participate in each other's lives. Based upon this starting point in the family, our equality as men and women expands into every dimension of life.

What is a "blessed family"?

A blessed family is one in which the parents have participated in the Marriage Blessing Ceremony. They affirm that marriage comes from God through True Parents, that they will be faithful to each other forever, that they will raise their children to be pure, and that they will share the Blessing with others. We offer the Marriage Blessing to any couple who understands this and takes the responsibility to fulfill it.

To find out more about the Marriage Blessing and how to receive it, contact our Blessing and Family Ministry at blessingamerica.

What are "blessed children"?

Blessed children are the progeny of couples who have received the Marriage Blessing. The Blessing changes the family's lineage from Satan's to God's, and so to us, "blessed" means to be released from Satan's claim due to the Fall of Adam and Eve. Blessed children are not born mature, and they of course have a personal responsibility to grow and become people of integrity and love. We support our blessed children, as we support all people, to choose a life of goodness and purity in body and soul.

Morality

What is the meaning of "absolute sex"?

Absolute sex means that the male-female principle is woven into the design of the universe, and that we should abide by this design as man and woman. It is the opposite of "free sex," for it calls us to uphold sexual purity before marriage and faithfulness to one partner in marriage.

Absolute sex means that when we live by God's design for husband and wife, we become God's temples. Our reproductive organs, the place where husband and wife become one in heart and body, are the place where, in true love, we achieve oneness with the Creator of the universe.

Did sin come from Adam and Eve eating a fruit? If not, then from where?

The Bible states that the original sin was Adam and Eve eating a fruit. (Gen 2) Father Moon affirms this, but asks, based on the Bible, was it a literal fruit? To say so contradicts Jesus' words that what goes into the mouth does not defile you. (Mt 15:11) God told Adam they would die if they ate it, but no parent of love would put a poisonous fruit in their child's reach. No parent of love would kill His children over a matter of disobedience, and banish all their offspring over it. So we do not believe it was a literal fruit.

So what was it? It was something so tempting that Adam and Eve risked death to have it. It was something that turned them from being innocently naked to hiding their lower parts. We conclude that it was a sexual relationship, one that they engaged in selfishly, with no connection to God, and felt guilty about. Wrongful man-woman love is the sin of the first parents; it caused their spiritual death. This explains why their mistake affected their children. It sheds light on the struggles we all have with sexuality, and on the corruption of love we see in the world around us.

How does the Family Federation protect young people from free sex?

To protect young people from free sex, the FFWPU promotes family life, faith formation and community education. An intact home with a father and mother is the best way to protect from free sex. Thus, a pro-family culture with good parental standards is the key to the purity of youth as well as adults.

In each step of upbringing, we respect our body as God's temple. We teach self-discipline and life for others. Our families share God's words and prayer in home worship, and our communities promote our values through the Women's Federation for World Peace, American Clergy Leadership Conference, Collegiate Association for the Research of Principles and Universal Peace Federation. We also work collegially with like-minded organizations.

Do Unificationists believe we can end evil and corruption in this world?

Yes, we do. To overcome a world of evil and corruption God has revealed a new truth that embraces and harmonizes historical religions, science and philosophy, and allows all people to know the reality of God and life after death. When one feels the reality of God, the conscience comes alive and guides one on the path to happiness, free from sin and wrongdoing. This new truth, as taught by Father and Mother Moon, stands on the foundation of all religions.

What is the Unificationist view on homosexuality and same-sex marriage?

We affirm that those with same-sex attraction are children of God who offer much to the world, and we strive to love and understand everyone. Nonetheless, we consider that homosexuality is not part of God's design for us. We look at the world and see a pair system composed of complementary plus-minus, or male-female partners. We see life and beauty growing out of this partnership. This natural pattern confirms the biblical revelation in Genesis 1:27, that God's image is male and female. Social science tells us that families led by the biological mother and father bring overwhelming benefits, both for the individual and society as a whole. Hence in order to more fully resemble God and fulfill His love in our own marriage relationships, and build a peaceful and happy world, the marriage Blessing in our tradition is between a man and a woman.

Death and Eternal Life

What happens to us after we die?

After we die, our finite body is given back to the earth and our spirit ascends to the spirit world, the eternal realm of love. Our passage into the spirit world is a new birth, like our arrival in this physical world from the womb. Our source of life on earth is air, sunlight and water, but in the spirit world, our source of life is love.

The quality of our life on earth determines our place in the spirit world. If we grow our spirit on earth through giving and receiving authentic love, we will find joy in heaven. We will meet the people whom we love and who love us, and experience eternal happiness together with God. If we live a selfish life on earth, we will not enjoy such happiness. God does not decide where we go in the spirit world; rather the way we live on earth determines our destination. Heaven and Hell are simply the realms closer to or further from God, our Heavenly Parent.

Do Unificationists believe in spirit world? Are there such things as spirits and "ghosts"?

Yes, we believe there is a spirit world. It is the place where our spirit body goes once our physical body passes away. Hence, spirits and "ghosts" are real; they are persons who departed this earth in times past.

The interaction between spirits and people on earth is also real. A spirit person can influence us, both for good and bad. A heavenly spirit can give us energy, inspiration and healing. A troubled or evil spirit, sometimes called a ghost, can drain our energy and introduce unwelcome feelings. Our faith in God, positive outlook, and strong bonds of love with family and friends enables us to maintain a healthy spiritual life.

Do Unificationists believe in heaven and hell?

Yes, we believe the spirit world includes both heaven and hell. These are realms closer to or further from the love of God and others. Where we enter the spirit world corresponds to our life on earth.

On earth and in the spirit world, we are created to dwell in the kingdom of heaven, where there is no shadow of wrongdoing. That is a world built upon love that is true, unselfish and unconditional. But the human Fall has bestowed fallen nature upon us. It tells us to ignore God, forget our responsibility, dominate others and multiply evil. By doing this, we create realms of hurt, anger, pain, lust and so forth in the spirit world. Those realms are referred to as hell. These realms will dissipate when God's salvation is fulfilled on earth.

How do Unificationists conduct memorial services?

We in the Unificationist tradition hold an ascension ceremony for those who have passed. It is called the "Seonghwa Ceremony." It can stand alone, or provide spiritual support for the memorial service of any faith tradition. "Seong" is a Korean word for sacred or holy. It tells us that the time of transition is a serious but joyful event, in which we should celebrate a person's birth into the third and final stage of their life.

As Father Moon explains, "The moment of entry into the spirit world is the time when we enter the world of ecstasy and victory. It is the moment we embrace the fruit of our life. It is a moment that comes only once. In that moment, others should congratulate us as much as they desire and then send us off. In that moment, they should shed tears of joy, not tears of sadness."

The Seonghwa normally takes place on the third day after the person ascends. We come together as a community in remembrance, celebration and support for the departed's family.

God, Christ and the Second Advent

Salvation and Resurrection

Do Unificationists believe in the resurrection?

Yes, we believe in the resurrection of Jesus two-thousand years ago, and in the resurrection of all people. As Jesus shows us, resurrection comes by giving one's life for one's enemies. Through the cross, Father Moon teaches, "Jesus triumphed over Satan and broke all his chains. … through this forty-day period of his resurrection, Jesus opened the way to redeem humanity's sins."

Hence we define resurrection as the process of being restored from spiritual death, far from God, to spiritual life in the love of God. Accordingly, whenever we repent of our sins and rise to a higher state of goodness, we are resurrected to that degree. Our resurrection comes on the basis of our ancestors' merit, our belief in God's Word, and our real life practice based on His guidance.

Do Unificationists believe in reincarnation?

We do not believe in reincarnation, but we do believe that "spirits who could not complete their mission must return to people on earth who share the same type of mission." This being the case, "from the standpoint of mission, the physical self of the person on earth concurrently serves as the physical self of the spirit. In a sense, he is the second coming of the spirit; hence he may sometimes be called by the spirit's name and appear to be the reincarnation of that spirit." In the Bible, Jesus called John the Baptist "Elijah" for this reason. We call this, "returning resurrection," and it explains the phenomena called "reincarnation."

Can we be saved and go to heaven?

Yes we can, and the condition that gets us to heaven is a life that has been lived for the sake of others, that is, a life of true love. A life of true love means, in Father Moon's words, "you perfect a true family, consisting of three generations living together in true love. In such families, the kingdom of heaven on earth takes root. If you do this while you are on earth, you will be eligible to enter heaven." So the heaven we go to, then, is "a world overflowing with God's true love." This heaven begins here on earth within families brought into the complete dominion of God through the marriage Blessing of True Parents.

Do Unificationists believe in eternal punishment?

Father Moon did not teach eternal punishment. Nonetheless, he did teach that if you live apart from God on earth, you will live apart from God in the spirit world. Those who have lived the farthest from God while on earth end up in realms dominated by selfishness, anger, resentment, guilt and the like. This is the place called hell. But this is not God's punishment; we weave our own fate. As Jesus said, what is bound on earth is bound in heaven. But God is ever seeking a relationship with you and me, as we, deep inside, are seeking for God. Therefore, hell is not eternal. Under the right conditions, our true love on earth resurrects those suffering in hell. As the Bible says in Hebrews 11:39-40, "apart from us spirit people should not be made perfect."

Second Coming

Is Jesus going to come again? If so, how?

Yes, Jesus is going to come again. Jesus clearly foretold his return, and he said that its time, place and manner will be revealed to the faithful.

Jesus coming on the clouds is unacceptable to the scientific mind. Some believe that the Second Advent occurs whenever Jesus comes to dwell within the heart, but Jesus has been dwelling within the hearts of faithful believers for millennia. Others teach that the Second Coming is Jesus' return as a spirit, but Jesus has always visited Christians in the spirit.

Father Moon presents a biblical alternative. The prophet Malachi foretold that Elijah would come down from heaven, but Jesus said that John the Baptist was Elijah. In like manner, Christ could be born on earth. In fact, in the Bible, God never sent a person on the clouds. Every single prophet, saint, and the Messiah himself, was born on earth.

We believe the Second Coming will not be on the clouds, and is more than an event in the heart or in the spirit. To redeem our sins, Christ must come in the flesh, on the earth.

Do Unificationists believe that Reverend and Mrs. Moon are the Second Coming?

Yes, we do. We believe that at the time of the Second Coming, God is embodied in True Parents, a true husband and wife who open the path by which all men and women may resurrect as true husbands and wives.

In the speech, "True Family and I," Mother Moon announced in scores of cities around the world, "Centering on the love of the True God, my husband and I are cleansing all the polluted elements that originated in the false family formed through false marriage. Through true love, we have purified the world of conscience and the spirit world. By doing so, we have achieved True Parents' position. Thus we are able to sow the seed of True Love, the seed of True Life, and the seed of True Lineage, which signifies the unity between God and human beings, to the couples participating in the marriage Blessing, the ceremony of resurrection."

This is our faith.

Will the Second Coming end evil and bring a world of peace?

We believe that by living for others in the family's school of love, free from the sin of the first parents, we will gradually vanquish all sin. Father Moon explained: "The Messiah will choose a woman in the position of the Mother based on the foundation of God's original love. They will set the condition to return to our hometown, the place of God's original love, on the level of the individual to the levels of family, tribe, people, nation and world."

True Parents and their family restored God's true love in this world. They offer this to us through the marriage Blessing. It frees all races, nations and religions to cooperate through projects such as the Peace Road, peace zones, humanitarian service and moral education, to bring a world of peace.

Jesus

Do Unificationists believe that Jesus died for our sins?

Father Moon taught that Jesus died for our sins. The blood he shed on the cross has given spiritual rebirth, salvation, and peace to people for centuries. According to Father Moon's Exposition of the Divine Principle, "God handed over Jesus to Satan as the condition of indemnity to save all humankind …God thus opened the way for all humanity to be engrafted with the resurrected Jesus and thereby receive spiritual salvation and rebirth." It goes on to say, "Jesus came with love and sacrifice to give all that he had to humankind, even offering his life. If we turn to him in faith, we will 'not perish but have eternal life.'"

That having been said, we point out that Jesus forgave sins on earth. He did not have to go to the cross to do that. If the people had believed in him as Jesus asked them to, he would have married with God's Blessing, created a true family and brought forth the literal kingdom of God in his day.

Do Unificationists believe in the Virgin Birth?

Unificationists do not believe in a literal Virgin Birth, but do strongly affirm that the conception of Jesus was free of any trace of sin. Father Moon taught, "In order for Jesus to be born on earth and emerge as the Messiah, there had to be no condition for Satan's accusation, even from the time Jesus was in his mother's womb." The biblical account of Jesus' lineage reveals how God's worked to create His Son on earth. The account culminates in Luke 1, in which we read about Mary dwelling in the house of the high priest Zechariah for three months, where she became pregnant.

Do Unificationists believe there is salvation through Jesus' death on the cross?

We affirm salvation through the cross, and explain what it means in a very important way. Father Moon taught that Jesus came to bring full salvation. Full salvation releases us from sin in both spirit and flesh. Had the people believed in and followed Jesus, he would have granted them spiritual and physical salvation.

Yet the people did not believe in Jesus. Jesus' physical body was exposed to Satan's assault, and he was killed. As a result, while all believers in Jesus, and the world as a whole, have received the benefit of spiritual salvation, the ministry of actually saving the physical world was delayed until the Second Advent.

Do Unificationists believe Jesus should have married and had children?

Father Moon teaches that Jesus should have married and had children. The Bible calls Jesus the "last Adam" and the "second man," with Adam as the first. Adam had a bride, Eve. They were created to be fruitful in character and multiply children, and this was Jesus' destiny. John the Baptist referred to Jesus a bridegroom and Jesus referred to himself as the bridegroom. He said that the coming kingdom would be like a wedding banquet. The book of Revelation at the end of the Bible prophesies that the kingdom comes through the marriage of the Lamb, the Messiah.

Even without referring to the Bible, it is common sense that an ideal world begins with ideal families, families in which husbands and wives love each other faithfully, parents and children are one, and brothers and sisters live together in harmony with the natural world. The Messiah is simply the one who, with his bride, inaugurates such families, beginning with their own.

Why did Jesus say he would come again? And how should we expect him to appear?

Jesus said he would come again in order to complete the mission of the Messiah. This mission is clear from the prophets, from the account of Jesus' birth, and from his own words. It was to make us perfect as our Heavenly Father is perfect, and to inaugurate the kingdom of Heaven on earth.

There is no hint of two comings of the Messiah in prophecy. Jesus introduced this idea when it was clear that the people of his time, including his family and disciples, were not receiving him.

In order to restore us to perfect freedom and establish God's kingdom on earth, the Messiah will be born as Jesus was, of a woman, on earth. Just as the Old Testament prophecies of a coming in the sky were symbolic, New Testament prophecies of Jesus coming in the clouds are symbolic. In his teachings, Jesus made it clear that he would return as a man born on earth.

Did Jesus appear to Rev. Moon? What was Rev. Moon's experience?

Yes, in 1935, on Easter Sunday morning, Jesus appeared to Father Moon. In his words, "I was begging God in tears for answers. After I had spent the night in prayer, Jesus appeared before me. He appeared in an instant, like a gust of wind, and said to me, 'God is in great sorrow because of the pain of humankind. You must take on a special mission having to do with Heaven's work.' I saw clearly the sorrowful face of Jesus. I heard his voice clearly. The experience caused my body to shake violently. I was simultaneously overcome with fear and gratitude.

"Jesus spoke clearly about the work I would have to do. My initial response was, 'I can't do this.' I was truly afraid. I wanted somehow to avoid this mission, and I clung to the hem of his clothing and wept.

"My encounter with Jesus changed my life. His sorrowful expression was etched into my heart as if it had been branded there. I immersed myself completely in the Word of God. I experienced a series of days like these that led me into a deeper and deeper world of prayer. I embraced new words of truth that Jesus was giving me directly and let myself be completely captivated by God. I had many things to think about, and gradually became of boy of few words."

Messiah

What is the Unificationist definition of the Messiah?

Our definition of the Messiah is a person that has been anointed by God to fulfill God's providence of salvation: to build heaven on earth and enable all people to reach full maturity. Father Moon teaches that the Messiah is not only a man: "…there has to be an anointed daughter. The only begotten Son and Daughter would love and marry each other at the place where all can rejoice with God. Then, as the True Parents, they would give birth to children on earth."

Do Unificationists believe Reverend Moon is the Messiah?

Yes, Unificationists believe Sun Myung Moon, together with his wife, Hak Ja Han Moon, are the Second Coming of Christ. This means that they have become the embodiment of God's parental heart and love on earth. We believe that Jesus called Sun Myung Moon to this mission, the mission of Christ, to fulfill the purpose of God's creation of Adam. Adam's mission was to be a true son, true elder brother, true husband and true father to all generations. Adam's fall put all generations under Satan, so the Messiah as Savior has to buy them back, as Jesus did on the cross. The Messiah as True Parent takes his prepared bride and proceeds as one body with her to become a true husband and True Parents, give complete salvation by restoring us as couples, to the life, love and lineage of God. This salvation extends to our families, to the world, and to heaven and earth.

Why do Unificationists have the term "tribal messiah"? What does it mean?

A "tribal messiah" is a couple that receives God's grace through the marriage Blessing and takes responsibility to share it with others. The Blessing liberates marriage from the sin of the first parents, and empowers us to liberate others. We begin by serving the needs, wants and interests of our family and friends, and those to whom God guides us. The ultimate service we can give is to share God's Word and Blessing. In this way, we are messiahs, with a small "m," through whom the Spirit of God builds communities of goodness that expand across the world.

Heavenly Parent

Why do Unificationists call God, "Heavenly Parent"?

We call God "Heavenly Parent" in order to honor the Genesis 1 image of God as male and female. Father Moon pointed out that God is the source of the pair system, composed of male and female, throughout the universe. We conclude, in harmony with the "yin-yang" understanding of eastern traditions, that God possesses both a masculine nature and feminine nature. Semitic religions have called God Heavenly Father in recognition of God's masculinity, and at the same time the Mosaic Law calls all people to honor both father and mother; prophets such as Hosea depict God's motherly heart, and Paul refers to "the Jerusalem above" as "our mother." In this age we can begin to grasp God's femininity and the value of true womanhood. We express this through the term, Heavenly Parent.

How can we know that God is our Parent?

Unificationists understand several ways that we can know God is our Parent. We see Heavenly Parent through the order and beauty of creation, in which all things multiply their kind, generation upon generation, through Christ-like sacrificial love prevailing through suffering at the hands of evil in human history, and through our heart when we love as God loves, totally for others. By going beyond ourselves in service to others, Father Moon said, we will meet God as our Parent. Parents give endlessly to their children, and wish they could give more. Parents want their children to be greater than they are. This is the God we know.

Do Unificationists believe God is a Trinity, the Father, Son and Holy Spirit?

Father Moon's teachings affirm the Trinity, which means that God is one-in-three and three-in-one. He explained this in terms of God's nature and God's presence in the world.

In terms of God's nature, Exposition of the Divine Principle teaches that "God is the harmonious union of masculinity and femininity ... God is the one absolute reality in whom the dual characteristics interact in harmony; therefore, He is a Being of the number three."

In terms of God's presence in the world, Exposition states "Jesus and the Holy Spirit stand as [male and female] object partners of God. They unite through give and take with each other with God as the center. God, Jesus and the Holy Spirit thus become one, and this oneness constitutes the Trinity." Building upon this, we believe that each man and woman is created to marry and live as a trinity with God as the center.

Pillars of Unificationism

Our Scriptures

What do Unificationists believe about the Bible?

We believe that God reveals His Word and His central providence in the Bible. Father Moon's teachings, the Divine Principle, provide a logical and practical explanation of the Bible for today's world. It sets forth principles by which we can resolve conflicting views of the Bible, and clarify the Bible's stories of humankind's origin, Noah, Abraham, Moses and Israel, Jesus and the Second Coming. Everything in the Bible provides guidance for our individual lives and the whole world.

What are the Unificationist Holy Scriptures?

We believe that the scriptures of all religions are holy. From our tradition, Father Moon designated eight "great textbooks." They are The Sermons of the Rev. Sun Myung Moon, Exposition of the Divine Principle, Cheon Seong Gyeong ("Heavenly Scripture"), The Family Pledge, Pyeong Hwa Shin Gyeong ("Peace Scriptures"), True Families—Gateway to Heaven, Owner of Peace and Owner of Lineage and World Scripture.

The first "text" is 600+ volumes long, and the last is a two-volume compilation of texts from the scriptures of the world's religions. Father Moon also had as much faith in his autobiography, As a Peace-Loving Global Citizen, as in these texts, and said that he was waiting for "a second or third volume of Cheon Seong Gyeong."

After Father Moon's passing, Mother Moon guided the publication of a new edition of Cheon Seong Gyeong, an expansion of Pyeong Hwa Shin Gyeong, which includes the fourth through seventh texts on the list of eight, and an account of True Parents' life and works, Chambumo Gyeong (True Parents' Scripture).

Is the ultimate truth found in a book? If not, then where?

The ultimate truth is not found in a book. Words are a means of expressing the truth and are not the ultimate truth itself. Jesus said that the people sought to find life in the scriptures, but the scriptures were simply a testimony to him. He said that if they came to him, then they would find life.

The truth, the life, is found in a true man and true woman. Jesus, a true man, said that he was the way and the truth and the life. We affirm this, and affirm that through the marriage Blessing, we ourselves, men and women, can become the way, the truth and the life. And Father Moon added one more term: the love.

True Father Sun Myung Moon

Who is Sun Myung Moon?

Born in 1920, Sun Myung Moon emerged from a Korean farming village to attain global stature. After founding the Holy Spirit Association for the Unification of World Christianity in 1954, he launched organizations for dialogue and alliance across all boundaries, centered on God and true family life. In his words, "I went down thorny paths utterly alone. Not even God could acknowledge me. I endured imprisonment six times, though I was innocent. My life has been for the sake of perfecting the model of absolute conjugal love and the ideal family. I have endured for the sake of our God, who deserves pity, and for the world's people who are suffering." Thereby Father Moon "opened wide the path for people to reach full spiritual maturity and establish true families, true clans, true nations, and a true world, by leading lives of true love."

How did God work in Father Moon's life?

God worked in Father Moon's life as a Heavenly Parent with a son of absolute filial piety. Father Moon grasped that God is like a father who labored and sweated his entire life for his children, only to have a thief steal everything in one night. God revealed to him at a young age His sorrowful, painful heart. God showed him that the only way for a Heavenly Parent of love to recover His children was to love his enemies more than He loved His children, and to gather people who would follow that ethic.

Thus God allowed Father Moon to suffer persecution on His behalf, as an individual, as a family and to the global level. When He saw Father Moon absorb the blows and pray for those who attacked him, God blessed him. God blessed him because, in Father Moon's words, "I applied the values of a life of true love, emerged triumphant, and offered that triumph to humanity. I recovered a parent-child relationship between God and humankind, and opened the way of rebirth in the lineage of God."

When did he die, and what happened after that?

After an extended bout with respiratory failure, Father Moon died on September 3, 2012 (July 17 by the Lunar, or Heavenly, Calendar). He was 92. Two weeks later Mother Moon led his memorial service–the Seonghwa Ceremony–attended by hundreds of thousands at the Peace World Center, an indoor stadium on the church campus at Cheongpyeong, Korea. He was interred on the grounds of the Peace Palace at Cheongpyeong. It was four months before Foundation Day, the establishment of the substantial Kingdom of God (Cheon Il Guk). True Parents, Father Moon in Heaven and Mother Moon on earth, with the global movement, celebrated this day.

Together with her husband in spirit, Mother Moon is advancing True Parents' mission. She continues translation of his teachings, the formation of a constitution, the expansion of tribal messiahship and the marriage Blessing, and preparation of young leadership. Mrs. Moon calls members to deepen the spirit of familial love in local community life. Through a period of organizational development, Mother Moon has maintained patience and kindness and called upon all to forgive, love and unite.

Do Unificationists believe that Sun Myung Moon is the Messiah?

We believe that Father Moon is the Messiah, the Savior and True Parent of Heaven, Earth and all Humankind. This sounds overwhelming but it is actually simple. In fact, when a scholar asked him if he were the Messiah, Father Moon answered, yes, and you should be the Messiah too.

We believe that Jesus called Sun Myung Moon to this mission, the mission of Christ, to fulfill the purpose of God's creation of Adam. Adam's mission was to be a true son, true elder brother, true husband and true father to all generations. Adam's fall put all generations under Satan, so the Messiah as Savior has to ransom them back, as Jesus did on the cross. The Messiah as True Parent takes a bride and proceeds in oneness with her to become a true husband and True Parents, recognized by the world that receives God's Word and marriage Blessing from them. We proclaim that Father and Mother Moon, with their family of three generations and clergy of the world's religions, accomplished this for all time, breaking down the gates of hell and opening the gates of God's kingdom.

True Mother Hak Ja Han Moon

What is the role of Mrs. Moon in the Family Federation?

Mother Moon is our co-founder and central figure on earth, working as one with Father Moon in Heaven. We believe that when true love unites the husband, wife and God as one through the marriage Blessing, no force in the universe can break this apart.

Mother Moon said, "when husband and wife become one, their union symbolizes the unity of heaven and earth. When husband and wife are in unity based on God's love, the way to bring the absolute and inseparable oneness of all humankind with God, and unity in the universe, opens up."

Thus Mother Moon's authority is that of a co-creator. She manifests God's love and truth as a true wife in eternal oneness with her husband.

After his passing, she continues the mission together with men and women of good-will throughout the world.

How many children and grandchildren do she and Rev. Moon have?

Father and Mother Moon have fourteen children and thirty-seven grandchildren (and counting). But just as important are their spiritual offspring, the hundreds of thousands of men and women who have engrafted into God's love, life and lineage through the Marriage Blessing.

Do Unificationists consider Mother Moon the co-founder? Do you have married couples in leadership?

Yes, Father and Mother Moon are the co-founders of the Family Federation. Just as a family cannot come into being without a father and mother, so too the Family Federation could not come into being without a father and mother. For all couples, we teach that husband and wife together inherit and share the rights of equal participation, position and ownership, eternally. Echoing the words of Genesis 2 and Matthew 19, through marriage blessed by God, husband and wife become one.

Following their example, and our knowledge that a man or woman alone can only be one half of the whole, our ideal is for positions of leadership to belong to blessed couples. For us, leadership, educating and parenting go together.

True Parents

What does the term, "True Parents," mean? Why is it so important?

True parents are a husband and wife who, based on their personal maturity and God's Blessing, unite God's love with their love. Their love is God's dwelling place on earth. In Father Moon's words, True parents "determine the standard of value of all that is in motion in heaven and on earth. They are the measure of value that is the hope of all beings. This is true because God is such a being." The first true parents are the perfected ancestors of all humankind, so we capitalize the term in their case.

This is important because Adam and Eve were meant to be those True Parents, but they fell. Because we have not had True Parents, we have suffered apart from God, and we could not become true husbands and wives and true parents ourselves. Jesus and the Holy Spirit are our spiritual True Parents. On their foundation, God called Sun Myung Moon and Hak Ja Han Moon to be substantial True Parents, to lead us into blessed marriage and completely vanquish sin and suffering.

Can any married couple become "true parents"?

Every married couple can, must and someday will become true parents. Father Moon said, "I ask you to follow my example. I began this work for a reason. Jesus walked the tragic path of death to resolve this issue, and God suffered through six thousand providential years to resolve it. The path I am walking differs from yours only in scale and scope. My path is at the national and world levels, but in essence it is the same as yours. There is no difference in terms of what you and I should do in our lives."

In the Blessing vow, couples commit to establish a family in which God dwells, and to bring their children and all people, beyond nation, race and religion, to receive the marriage Blessing. By God's grace, fulfilling this makes us true parents.

How does a person receive True Parents?

A person receives True Parents through the marriage Blessing. We prepare for this by making a foundation. Father Moon taught how people and nations have made these foundations throughout history, and how this applies to our lives today.

The foundation begins with offering something to God, based on faith, for a period of time. You can offer the things of creation, prayer, study of the Word, service, your physical body by fasting, and so forth.

A period of time for doing so, for example, 40 days, is part of the offering. The foundation also means that you bring the spirit you have developed into mentoring and loving others with the heart of a parent, winning their respect and trust. By these steps, you gain the maturity that leads to successful marriage and your own true parenting.

Do Unificationists worship True Parents?

No, we do not. The word we use for our relationship with True Parents is "attend." To attend means, out of gratitude for what they have done for us and for all people, to keep that person in your heart, and to share common purposes and values in a relationship of love and respect. Attendance entails filial piety, loyalty, fidelity, faith, sacrificial service and benevolence. We do find God in True Parents. We also find God in our spouse, our parents, our children, all people and in nature. Most importantly, we find God in our conscience.

Unification Church

When was the Unification Church founded, and why?

Father Moon, with five disciples, established the Holy Spirit Association for the Unification of World Christianity, known as the Unification Church, on May 1, 1954 in Seoul, Korea. He said, "after Korea's liberation, I wanted to make a new beginning together with Christianity, but because of opposition from ministers, that was blocked. After that, I was supposed to work with Korea, but that road also was blocked."

Father Moon had to build his own institutional foundation to fulfill Christianity's mission. That mission was to overcome Communism and the breakdown of youth morality, to unite the world's religions, to restore values to science, the arts and media, to establish true God-centered marriages, and to proclaim the Second Advent of Christ in True Parents.

Did the Unification Church start a worldwide movement?

Yes, the Unification Church started a worldwide movement. It grew from a house church in Korea, to 120 churches within six years, to 120 countries in 22 years, to virtually all nations in forty years.

Putting our vision into practice, members developed affiliated organizations to apply God-centered values to academia, religion, race relations, governance, family and community formation, business, oceanic development, science, and the arts and media. Many of these organizations established chapters and activities for the sake of peace and human betterment throughout the world.

Is the Unification Church a cult?

No, it is not a cult, as the word is commonly understood. It began as a new religious movement that expanded rapidly and called for radical change, and whose members lived their beliefs. The establishment felt threatened and responded by labeling it a danger, and "cult" is the word for "danger" in the West.

Father Moon's teaching in Exposition of Divine Principle puts this in historical perspective: "The new age sprouts and grows amidst the final phases of the old age and comes into conflict with that age. Accordingly, it is difficult for a person steeped in the old tradition to understand or accept the new providence. Jesus, for example, came in such a way as to bewilder the faithful adherents of the Mosaic Law."

Society struck Jesus, as it does all saints and prophets, and it struck Father Moon. Our response is to absorb the "cult" persecution and keep on loving.

Family Federation for World Peace and Unification

What is the Family Federation for World Peace and Unification (FFWPU)? Is it a religion?

The Family Federation for World Peace and Unification, inaugurated on July 30, 1996, is best understood as a worldwide para-religious movement. Religion traditionally places the salvation of the individual at the center, and we support all religions in this mission. Our goal builds upon that to the salvation of the family unit. Our goal is to build true families through the holy marriage Blessing, and on that foundation to create communities, nations and a world of peace.

How is the Family Federation organized?

FFWPU families meet regularly to pray, read and reflect on True Parents' words, fellowship, educate children and youth, share the Holy Marriage Blessing, and offer service and friendship to the larger community. All religions can prepare people to create true marriages and families, and so the community of any and every religion, be it a parish, congregation, synagogue, masjid, temple or family church, can participate in the Family Federation. Father Moon envisioned that, based on the principles of true love, the kingdom of heaven on earth is nothing other than the community life of blessed families of peace.

What do you have to do to belong to the Family Federation?

The path to membership in the Family Federation begins with mentoring and education in preparation for the holy marriage Blessing. On that foundation, as couples we receive the Blessing, at which point we become Family Federation members. Belonging then means that a couple upholds the Family Pledge in community with other blessed families, striving to perfect the family ideal of true love. As husband and wife, Father Moon asked us to "pledge that you will live your life with gratitude and in eternal service to your spouse," and promised, "God will dwell eternally in such families and, with them at the center, the world-level family will begin to multiply."

What is the meaning of "home church"?

Home church means that the love in our family overflows in service and blessing to our neighbors. It begins with simple care and friendship. In Father Moon's words, "you love others as parents and share the truth and the heavenly moral standard." He envisioned that every home can be like a church, temple, synagogue or mosque, a dwelling place of God through authentic love within families that overflows into the community. As home churches link across the globe, he envisioned, it will create "an unbreakable chain of love, directly sustained by the Holy Spirit."

What is the "Family Pledge"?

The Family Pledge is a covenant and guideline for blessed families, Rev. Moon proclaimed it on May 1, 1994. Its eight short verses convey the blessings, mission and responsibilities of the family. Father Moon said, "You offer the Family Pledge to God the Creator, our Heavenly Parent, and the True Parents. Beyond that, you recite the Family Pledge to bring all families across the world to God." He asked us to recite the Pledge as a family, just as he did with his family. The Pledge expresses the highest ideals for the family, from which begins "everything in heaven and on earth, such as happiness, freedom and peace."

What is the meaning of "True God's Day" and "Foundation Day"?

True God's Day is an annual celebration of God, our Creator and Heavenly Parent. It takes place on the first day of each new year, by the Lunar Calendar. Father and Mother Moon established this day in 1968, based on the foundation of their victorious family, their blessing of many families, and the national expansion of the Unification Church. It was the first day ever set aside to authentically honor the true God and offer each year to Him.

Over the decades, True Parents' ministry of teaching God's Word and giving God's marriage Blessing, carried out by their three-generation family, together with leaders of the world's religions and nations, was bestowed throughout heaven and earth. Apace with this, True Parents' own marriage Blessing ascended to the national and global levels and, with it, God was enthroned as King of all kings. Foundation Day, inaugurated in 2013, culminated this with the marriage Blessing of True Parents uniting Heavenly Parent with the earth. With Father Moon in spirit world and Mother Moon on earth, Cheon Il Guk, the nation of cosmic peace and harmony, was made substantial. Like True God's Day, Foundation Day is now an annual celebration.

Marriage Blessing

What is the marriage Blessing?

The marriage Blessing is the marriage ceremony bestowed by the True Parents. Similar to other traditions, it features vows and the exchange of rings, and is legally recognized when administered by a registered officiant. However, the Blessing is unique in that its main purpose is not simply to bring a man and a woman together who love each other, but to restore marriage and family life to the way God intended it to be.

We understand that God had a beautiful ideal for marriage and family, something that we yearn for but often do not experience. We believe that since the beginning of human history, God wanted for each of us to experience living in love, but we have been trapped by the sins of our first ancestors and have lived in a world that does not reflect God's ideal for us. Through the Blessing, couples come into God's lineage as direct sons and daughters, and this liberates us to create ideal families that stay together on earth and in heaven.

Do Unificationists practice arranged marriage?

The Family Federation affirms the practice of arranged marriage, as is found in many religious traditions, when it is based upon God's heart and Principle. Father Moon said that "If Adam and Eve had not fallen, when the right time came, God naturally would have brought them together in marriage." Following that design, we want God to guide us in marriage, and we believe that He works best through one's parents.

In the first decades of their ministry, Rev. and Mrs. Moon as the True Parents arranged marriages for tens of thousands of couples. Today we support young people taking an active role in finding a spouse in partnership with their parents. Parents know their children best, and they provide the perspective that, in Father Moon's words, "ideal things are to be found not in the here and now, but in the future." It is liberating to allow a parental heart to enter into this key area of life.

Why do Unificationists hold mass weddings?

We conduct mass weddings as a way to show that humankind is one family sharing a global culture of love. It is a peacebuilding process that helps resolve enmity between religions and nationalities, as people of different backgrounds come together to inaugurate and celebrate the process of family formation.

It has a practical purpose, as a way for Rev. and Mrs. Moon to minister to the tens of thousands around the world seeking their marriage Blessing.

And finally, there is a spiritual dimension. Adam and Eve's Blessing would have been a world-shaping event, and mass weddings are a way for each couple to help shape a new world with God.

Do Unificationists think the marriage Blessing frees people from sin?

The marriage Blessing frees us from the sin of the first parents, which has to do with their marriage and is the cause of all sins. We have this sin removed when we are reborn as husband and wife through the marriage Blessing. Satan's claim on marriage is removed.

The Blessing does not bring instant perfection. What it does is open a gate to the path of perfection that was never opened before. Each husband and wife now can step forward to fulfill the purpose of creation, even if we make mistakes along the way, knowing that God is always with us.

How does one prepare for the marriage Blessing?

The Family Federation provides education and mentoring as preparation for the marriage Blessing. We have three levels of Blessing education. Level 1 introduces the ideals, values and principles of marriage. Level 2 is for those who are beginning their personal path toward marriage. It provides step-by-step guidance about initiating the engagement process and bringing it to a successful conclusion. Level 3 teaches skills that create a joyful and life-giving marriage.

This curriculum is adaptable for use within all faith traditions. For more information, go to Matching Education.

What does the marriage Blessing ceremony consist of?

Once you understand the meaning of the marriage Blessing, you embark upon an enriching five steps. The first is for you and your spouse to receive God's grace through the Holy Wine Ceremony. Then comes the Wedding Ceremony itself, which includes the exchange of rings, prayer and a sprinkling with Holy Water.

Third, you and your spouse share the Indemnity Ceremony, to separate from sin and hurtful actions in the area of marital love. This leads to your forty-day period of spiritual renewal and Three-Day Ceremony of purification, prayer and love together with God.

If your parents were blessed, then you will participate in the second part, the Wedding Ceremony, only. The other steps are to separate from the inheritance of the past, which your parents' marriage Blessing covers.

Does the Family Federation encourage marriage beyond religion, race and nation?

Yes, absolutely. We believe that the cross-cultural marriage Blessing helps transcend the barriers of race, culture, nationality, ethnicity and religion to create one world-wide family.

When the children of enemy families join together through the cross-cultural Holy Marriage Blessing, love each other and build a happy home, the grandparents grow closer to each other. In time, lineages that were once enemies become friends. The family is the pattern for people to live together in harmony. With the grace of God's Blessing, we will see this become a pattern for nations to live together in harmony.

Identity and Lifestyle

About Unificationists

What is a Unificationist?

We are people of faith working together to build a better world. We participate in Unification family churches and communities as well as in all the world's faith traditions. We come from all backgrounds, races, ethnicities and nationalities, and strive to live as one family under God. We believe that God called Rev. Sun Myung Moon and his wife, Dr. Hak Ja Han Moon, to bestow the Holy Marriage Blessing, which liberates us all to build ideal families for world peace. We honor the world's great scriptures, and view Reverend Moon's teachings as an expression of the principles and ideals common to them all.

What do Unificationists believe?

The building block of our faith was Rev. Moon's prayerful search to find the cause of the sin of the first parents, Adam and Eve, and a way to reverse that sin and restore the world according to God's original plan. Reverend Moon dedicated his life to comforting God's heart. He discovered foundational principles, among them are that God is alive and is the Parent of humankind, that God's nature is true love, and that God will save the world through His substantial expression on earth, the True Parents.

We believe that God created the world and placed in it His children, Adam and Eve, for the purpose of everlasting joy through love. He created us male and female, and gave us three blessings: to reach maturity, receive His marriage Blessing, and create a beautiful family and world. Tragically, Adam and Eve succumbed to self-centered love, left God, and created a broken family that expanded into a world of evil and suffering.

To turn this around, on the foundation of the great religions, Jesus came as Messiah, the new Adam, to take a bride as the new Eve, become True Parents and fulfill God's three blessings. Jesus died alone, offering his life to save sinful human beings who did not recognize him. By God's power he resurrected from the grave and sent the Holy Spirit. To complete his mission, he called Rev. and Mrs. Sun Myung Moon to become True Parents and empower all people to fulfill God's three blessings.

We believe that God's love is embodied in the family which opens the way to peaceful and prosperous communities, beyond religion, race and nationality.

What is unique about Unificationists?

We are unique in having a husband and wife as co-founders. Our mission is to save families, not just individuals. We are set apart by our understanding that God called Sun Myung Moon and Hak Ja Han Moon to be True Parents, and to bestow the Holy Marriage Blessing to committed men and women of all faith traditions, as the foundation for creating world peace through God-centered families.

We uphold God, the Creator, whose kingdom begins with the family. God's love is embodied in blessed marriages and families, which open the way to peaceful and prosperous communities, beyond religion, race and nationality.

Are Unificationists Christians?

Unificationists are people, of any faith tradition, who have received the marriage Blessing of True Parents. The Blessing is not religious conversion, for it stands on and affirms the teachings of the world's great religions.

Rev. Moon was born and raised in a Confucian and Buddhist household that converted to Christianity when he was ten. As a devout Christian youth, he received his life mission from Jesus. He teaches that Jesus is the Son of God, prepared for through the Old Testament Age, who died for our sins. Jesus revealed the revolutionary truth that all people are God's children, one global family. Thus, the marriage Blessing is rooted in God's providence revealed in the Bible. Nonetheless, the Blessing affirms and stands on the foundation of all religions.

Faith

Does faith in God make sense amidst so much suffering in the world?

Yes, faith in God does make sense, even in a world of suffering. God is your spiritual Parent. He grieves over the suffering in the world, and over the suffering each of us goes through. Nonetheless, God created you with your own portion of responsibility. He will not take that away from you. So He will not interfere with the choices you make, even if they are wrong choices that lead to suffering.

God does not whisk suffering away, but rather invests love and guidance. He hopes that you will choose just as He does—to bring happiness to others. When each of us fulfills our responsibility to live for the sake of others, we will not have the suffering we see today.

Can we harmonize religion and science?

Through understanding God's principles by which He created the world, you can see within yourself the way to harmonize religion and science. You have two sides. One is the spiritual side that connects to religion. The other is the physical side that listens to science and understands the natural world. By connecting the spiritual and physical within you, you naturally will harmonize what you learn through religion and science.

Reverend Moon put this into practice on a larger level. He called scientists to apply spiritual values to their technical pursuits. He called them to apply a new ethic based on love for nature, respect for human beings, and a search for God. At the same time he called religious leaders to express their teachings in reasonable and plain language. He told them not to focus on their own religion's growth, but rather to serve other religions and the good of humankind.

What does religious faith have to do with academia, the media and governance?

Through each person's faith and understanding and in ways sometimes unknown, God connects to our world, including using venues such as academia, the media and government as a way to advance the greatest common good. God's truth, when fully understood and shared in love, applies to real world challenges. Rev. Moon sought to model this through his movement's practice. Major results of his inspiration in these arenas include the work of the Professors World Peace Academy, Washington Times Foundation and Universal Peace Federation.

The PWPA discusses the divine in relation to concrete problems and traditional theories. A PWPA conference in 1985, for example, called the West to prepare for the fall of the Soviet Empire. ProfWorldPeace The Washington Times Foundation promotes journalistic freedom and ethical responsibility. It sponsors forums for global leaders, who discuss problems such as the stalemate on the Korean Peninsula. WashTimesFdn The Universal Peace Federation's branches around the world conduct interfaith-based dialogue and community building for local and national leaders. UnivPeaceFed

How do you explain the existence of God?

In a way consistent with the tenets of all faiths, we provide logical answers and practical answers to explain the existence of God. To answer logically, we refer to the order and beauty of creation and to the order and direction of human history.

Our practical answer is to believe that God exists and live based on that belief. Talk to God in prayer. Give of yourself for others. Practice your religion's spiritual disciplines, and study its spiritual teachings. Find a good mentor, and be a mentor to others. We think that your experiences will confirm God's existence.

Religion

What is the purpose of religion?

The purpose of religion is to enable us to achieve oneness of mind and body centered on God. The world's religions, each inspired by God to serve a particular culture, provide us the path to subdue our physical desires and to strengthen the power of the mind, or spirit. In this way we separate from the evil that takes possession of us through the body and gain the freedom to live fully and completely for others. Religion thereby provides us the foundation of purity necessary for God to grant us the marriage Blessing that He intended for Adam and Eve. When all humankind fully receives this Blessing, religion will have fulfilled its purpose.

Why are there so many religions? How do we know which one is right?

There are many religions because God wanted to bring His ideals into diverse cultures. Adam and Eve's descendants scattered across the earth, developed different languages and character traits, and responded to God in different ways. God sent prophets and saints to every culture to found religions. He developed them through the original minds of those who sought the good.

Even though the expression of religious striving takes different forms, all religions share the same core elements and ideals. This is because the purpose underlying all religions is to seek the family that was lost in the Garden of Eden. Therefore, what makes a religion right is the degree to which it understands that God is our Parent and we are His children, and practices sacrificial love.

Will religions ever fulfill their high ideals?

Yes, they will. The God-centered family is the place where the ideals of all religions are fulfilled. Religions emerged in order to seek the family that was lost in the Garden of Eden. Accordingly, we share the Blessing ceremony with leaders and members of all religions. The marriage Blessing brings religions to set aside their differences and focus on the creation of ideal families. When religions bring forth families of all races, nations and religions centering on true love, true life and true lineage, their ideals will be fulfilled.

Health and Spirituality

How do Unificationists define spiritual growth? How does it come about?

Spiritual growth is very real. It takes you beyond selfishness and into life for others. It brings a natural desire to serve, to forgive, to care, to sacrifice for the benefit of others, even beyond your own religion, race and nation.

Spiritual growth happens in the same way as physical growth: through nourishment and exercise. Your nourishment is God's love and truth, received directly or indirectly, through scriptures, parents, teachers and mentors. Exercise means your physical body's good deeds, deeds that put God's love and truth into action. Together these bring spiritual growth.

Do Unificationists drink alcohol and smoke tobacco?

The Family Federation does not take a public position on the use of alcohol or tobacco. Instead we build a culture of living for others. No one smokes or drinks for the sake of others. Alcohol dulls the spirit, can provide false comfort, and too often contributes to vehicle accidents, bad moral decisions, and addiction. Smoking and drinking often bring on illnesses that burden one's spouse and children. These habits do not grow one's spirit nor strengthen family and community life.

Do Unificationists have special religious practices?

We endorse the spiritual disciplines of all the world's religions. We engage in and encourage all traditional spiritual practices: prayer and meditation, developing a daily and weekly spiritual rhythm, regular study of God's Word, active participation in the life of a spiritual community, service to others, receiving and giving mentoring, and most important, the practice of sexual purity. Individuals sometimes choose to invest in more strenuous spiritual practices, such as fasting, vigils and so forth.

A more internal, yet very important, spiritual practice for Unificationists is to substantiate love in personal relationships with spouse, parents and children. This ability to love expands to the community, nation, and world. We believe that the greatest spiritual practice is to love our enemy and win the heart of those who are different from us.

Do Unificationists believe in abortion and birth control?

Decisions about birth control and abortion require individual prayer and family consideration. In principle we choose life. We encourage husbands and wives to welcome all children they conceive. We strive to build stable families and homes that have the ability to welcome the children whom God gives us. We strive for sexual purity before marriage and fidelity within marriage.

From conception we embody the love, life and ideal of our parents. Therefore parents minister spiritually to the unborn child. As a community we pray for the health of every mother and child. We seek God's guidance and blessing upon every unique circumstance.

Humanitarian Service and Reconciliation

What are some ways Unificationists help the poor and needy?

We devote on a personal level to our neighbors and local community. Among such efforts, usually unseen, cleaning neighborhoods, family values education, and participation in food pantries and community events are common. We also work to help the poor and needy through organizations affiliated with the Family Federation. The International Relief Friendship Foundation provides relief to areas devastated by poverty, illness, natural disasters. IRFF information The Women's Federation for World Peace, a UN-NGO, works to empower women around the world to heal racial and religious divides, staff and fund schools, provide medical services, provide relief funds, strengthen families and teach strategies for peace and reconciliation. WFWP Other organizations for humanitarian service and reconciliation include the International Coalition for Religious Freedom ICRF and Middle East Peace Initiative MEPI. Unificationist youth education programs Generation Peace Academy GPA and Next Gen Academy NGA include annual overseas service projects.

How do Unificationists engage in interreligious dialogue?

From the beginning, Father Moon was active in the Korean Religious Association for dialogue among diverse faiths. In the 1970s, the Unification Theological Seminary founded the New Ecumenical Research Association (New ERA), which gathered Christian scholars in dialogue. The network expanded to the world's religions in the 1980s through the International Religious Foundation and its God Conference, Youth Seminar on World Religions, Interdenominational Conferences for Clergy, Assembly of the World's Religions and Council for the World's Religions.

In the 1990s, this congealed as the Inter-Religious Federation for World Peace, to address religious conflict and initiate collaborative relationships. The IRFWP is establishing inter-religious councils that serve municipalities, nations, and the United Nations. IRFWP

In the 2000s, Unificationists established the Middle East Peace Initiative (MEPI), which sponsored engagement among Jews, Palestinians and religionists from around the world, service projects, dialogues and interfaith pilgrimages to the Al Aqsa Mosque. MEPI

Father Moon's vision is expressed through World Scripture, a comparative anthology of sacred texts. World Scripture

Where have Unificationists achieved peace-building objectives?

In the 1960s and 70s, Unificationists in Korea and Japan conducted widespread educational work to inform all sectors of society of the falsehoods of communism. In the 1980s we did the same in Latin America, the United States and Germany. Dr. Thomas Ward documented the results. March to Moscow

Through the 80s, our interfaith conferences built bridges with Muslim scholars and clergy, which led to a 1991 conference in Alexandria, Egypt, at which key Islamic leaders decided the Gulf War was a secular, not religious conflict. We tried, unsuccessfully, to persuade American leadership to resolve the invasion of Kuwait through dialogue, not force of arms. Rev. Moon opened doors between the two Koreas through his meeting with Kim Il Sung in 1991 and built bridges of peace in the Middle East in the 2000s.

What is the Unificationist view concerning people with disabilities, handicaps and special needs?

We view people with disabilities, handicaps and special needs to be "treasures of heaven." Each is born for a purpose and can live a fulfilling life on earth and in heaven, including marriage and family life.

Since 2004, Unificationists in America have led the Treasures of Heaven ministry, to provide for the special needs population activities and programs for recreation and socialization. The ministry helps parents with a special needs child find healing through association with other parents in the same situation. It encourages mentoring and partnering with treasures of heaven children. You can find more information at Treasures of Heaven.

Peace Kingdom

Do Unificationists believe the earth can become the kingdom of God?

Yes, we believe the kingdom of God is possible on earth. Through connecting you and your family back to God's lineage through the Blessing and committing to a life of true love, this world can become the kingdom of God. Isaiah 46:11 says, "I have spoken and I will bring it to pass; I have purposed it and I will do it." The Fall destroyed the original world that God envisioned, but God has led providential history by bringing all people step by step to naturally surrender to the love and heart of God, our Heavenly Parent. When evil evaporates, the kingdom of God will naturally appear, because it is the original desire of God and of all people.

Is "Cheon Il Guk" a real place?

The foundation for Cheon Il Guk is real, but its complete manifestation will take time. Father Moon explained that this phrase means that God's kingdom is a nation where two that were separated become one. This starts with mind and body and expands to two people, two families, two clans or tribes, two ethnic groups, two nations, and the spiritual and physical worlds.

In his words, "Cheon Il Guk perfects the standard of a nation and ushers in the era of liberation and freedom, disconnected from all enmity." Father Moon taught that Cheon Il Guk will come through the Blessing of marriages between a husband and wife from enemy nations, religions or races. By imparting the Word and Blessing, Father and Mother Moon, with their family, disciples and ambassadors for peace, laid the real foundation for Cheon Il Guk in 180 nations.

What is the Universal Peace Federation?

The Universal Peace Federation (UPF), founded by Rev. and Mrs. Moon in 2005, is an international and inter-religious network of individuals and organizations, including representatives from religion, government, civil society and the private sector. I is an NGO in special consultative status with the Economic and Social Council of the United Nations. UPF supports the work of the United Nations, particularly in the areas of interfaith peacebuilding, peace education, and the strengthening of marriage and family.

UPF has five guiding principles: that we are one human family created by God; that the highest qualities of the human being are spiritual and moral; that the family is the school of love and peace; that we are created to live for the sake of others, and that peace entails cooperation beyond the boundaries of ethnicity, religion, and nationality.

What is the "Peace Road"?

The Peace Road was inspired by the International Highway Project (IHP), a visionary call for a super highway free of tariffs and passports, linking the entire globe. Father Moon first proposed it at the International Conference on the Unity of Sciences in 1981. It will be a global road and rail system that will not allow transport of munitions or armaments. Work began on the first link, the Japan-Korea undersea tunnel, on October 1, 1986. In his Peace Messages, delivered around the world in the 2000s, Father Moon called nations to lay down their arms and build another critical link, the Peace King Bridge and Tunnel across the Bering Strait, to connect the eastern and western hemispheres.

Mother Moon moved the project forward in 2015 by suggesting we take small steps throughout the world. Thus was born the Peace Road. In that year, traveling the Peace Road, cyclists toured their cities, states and regions to publicize the International Peace Highway in over 30 nations, from South Africa to Chile, Germany to Korea, and in 25 cities across America.

Politics

Are Unificationists more left wing or right wing? What does "headwing" mean?

We are neither left nor right wing, but are "headwing." Unificationist philosopher Dr. Sung Han Lee stated, "Unification Thought …is also called Godism or Head-Wing Thought. The term 'Godism' indicates that this system of thought has God's truth and love as its nucleus; … this system of thought is neither a part of the right wing nor of the left wing, but rather embraces both."

In Father Moon's words, "The headwing ideology …is the ideology of heart—the heart of a true child and the heart of a true spouse. You attend God as your Parent and maintain a family environment that builds blood ties with God," and by doing so "build the world of peace—the society of one human family centering on love." (see Headwing Thought)

Do Unificationists believe in freedom of religion?

We believe in freedom of religion. Unificationism teaches that people are created to relate with God in freedom, and to do so, "people in every age have been desperately crying out for freedom. …as aspirations for freedom mount in intensity, people will demand a social environment conducive to its realization. Revolutions will continue until true freedom has been fully restored."

Practicing this, Father Moon fought for freedom of religion in America. When persecuted for his faith, he declared himself "a representative of all those who have suffered government injustice, racial prejudice and religious bigotry. …I will fight till my last breath for religious liberty and the rights of minorities and the oppressed." To this end, in 1981 he founded the Coalition for Religious Freedom and, in 1984, the Common Suffering Fellowship.

What is Father Moon's concept for a world of peace?

Father and Mother Moon actively support the work of the United Nations. Together, they cast a vision for its future development. Their primary concern is not politics; it is to build a federation of families of peace that guide their nations. They called the UN to educate young people and families in this "Abel-like" direction, to bring God's blessings to the world and become an "Abel UN."

As a husband and wife who co-founded a global movement, they set the model for men and women serving together in global leadership. They perceived that women are "the central axis in building a new century characterized by a loving, peaceful culture." They called for women's leadership to renew the UN based on true family values. This would make it into an "Abel Women's UN." Father and Mother Moon thus set forth a balanced governing structure for a global family under God.

Womanhood

What is the Women's Federation for World Peace?

The Women's Federation for World Peace (WFWP) is a non-governmental organization (NGO) in general consultative status with the Economic and Social Council of the UN (UNESCO). It consists of a network of National WFWP Chapters in over 120 nations that are dedicated to empower women with the knowledge, the tools and the support needed to create peace at home, peace in our communities, our nations and throughout the world. Our WFWP in the United States expresses what we stand for in five statements:

- We affirm women's value in the eyes of a loving Creator, and promote a world of goodness and peace.

- We uphold and defend the God-given rights and dignity of women here in the United States and worldwide.

- We promote healthy and virtuous relationships within the

family between husband and wife, parents and children, and extended-family members, and we educate and nurture young women to develop a character of internal and external excellence.

- We embrace one global community transcending long-held barriers such as race, religion, and nationality through service, education, and celebration of unique differences.

- We empower women to take the lead for the sake of world peace in all sectors of society, utilizing their qualities of selflessness, compassion, and a desire for mutual prosperity that are central to a mother's heart.

What roles do women play in the Family Federation?

Women lead the Family Federation as daughters of Heavenly Parent, as wives, mothers and sisters, and in public roles. Men lead in the same way. We believe that husband and wife share in each other's lives and positions. Father and Mother Moon model this for all of us. They are Family Federation co-founders and, from a theological perspective, represent the masculinity and femininity of God.

What is the meaning of the "liberation of women" announced by Rev. and Mrs. Moon?

Women were critical to mission development globally, particularly in Africa and the Middle East, and to the leadership of the Unification Church in the United States. Women occupy leadership positions in major initiatives of the Unification movement, including the Women's Federation for World Peace, Cheongpyeong Heaven and Earth Training Center, Unification Theological Seminary, International Relief Friendship Foundation, and in our communities, regions, national and international offices.

Father and Mother Moon teach that the liberation of women means that the sin of Eve in the Garden of Eden is completely resolved. The explanation starts in the Bible. Remarkable women of Jesus' lineage separated themselves from evil to prepare the lineage from which the Son of God was born. Sarah, Rebekah, Leah and Rachel, Tamar and a succession of women repudiated Satan and upheld God's love at the cost of their lives. Father Moon discovered this and built upon it to receive Hak Ja Han as his bride.

From age 17, at the cost of her life, Hak Ja Han Moon stood with her husband to free men and women from the sin of the first parents through the marriage Blessing. After bearing 14 children, she emerged on the world stage and won the respect of world leaders and audiences including at the US Congress, the UN, and over 900 other venues. On this path of love, Mother Moon won the hearts of officials at Beijing's Great Hall of the People, which normally bans mention of God, and they invited her to share God's Word. Father Moon declared that by this and more, Mother Moon laid the foundation for the liberation of all women.

www.ingramcontent.com/pod-product-compliance
Lightning Source LLC
Chambersburg PA
CBHW052209110526
44591CB00012B/2138